CW00787821

THE
WORLD'S
TRAGEDY

OTHER NEW FALCON BOOKS!

Undoing Yourself With Energized Meditation
Secrets of Western Tantra
The Tree Of Lies
The Serpent, The Beast and The Golden Dawn (with Gary Ford)
    All By Christopher S. Hyatt, Ph.D.
The Way Of The Secret Lover
Enochian Sex Magick
Goetia And Sex Magick
    By C.S. Hyatt, Ph.D. and Lon DuQuette
Taboo: The Psychopathology Of Sex And Religion
    By Hyatt, DuQuette and Ford
Cosmic Trigger
Cosmic Trigger II
Quantum Psychology
    All By Robert Anton Wilson
Little Essays Toward Truth
Magick Without Tears
Equinox of The Gods
The Heart of The Master
The Worlds Tragedy
Eight Lectures On Yoga
AHA!
The Law Is For All
Gems From The Equinox
    By Aleister Crowley
Freedom Is A Two Edged Sword
    By Jack Parsons
Info-Psychology
Neuropolitque
    By Timothy Leary, Ph.D.
What You Should Know About The Golden Dawn
The Complete Golden Dawn System of Magic
    By Israel Regardie

And to get your free catalog of all of our titles, write to:

NEW FALCON PUBLICATIONS
Catalog Dept.
7025 E. 1ST Ave. Suite 5
SCOTTSDALE, AZ. 85251 U.S.A.

THE WORLD'S TRAGEDY

By
Aleister Crowley

Foreword By
Christopher S. Hyatt, Ph.D.
Lon Milo DuQuette

Introduction By
Israel Regardie

1991
NEW FALCON PUBLICATIONS
SCOTTSDALE, ARIZONA U.S.A.

COPYRIGHT © 1985 USESS

All rights reserved. No part of this book, in part or in whole, may be reproduced, transmitted, or utilized, in any form or by any means, electronic or mechanical, including photocopying, recording, or by any information storage and retrieval system, without permission in writing from the publisher, except for brief quotations in critical articles, books and reviews.

International Standard Book Number: 0-941404-18-8
International Standard Book Number: 1-56184-014-9

Library of Congress Catalog Card Number: 85-80865

First Edition 1910
Second Printing 1985, Falcon Press
Third Printing 1991 New Falcon Publications

Cover Concept: Christopher S. Hyatt, Ph.D.

NEW FALCON PUBLICATIONS
7025 E. 1st Ave. Suite 5
Scottsdale, Arizona 85251 U.S.A.
(602) 246-3546

DEDICATION

I owe this book as all that I possess, to my playmates in the Garden of Eros; but they are rich; they want for nothing; therefore I give it to the poor boys and girls of England, so that, shaking off morality and religion, they may be partakers in Love unto the glory of

PAN.

FALCON'S
LIMITED COLLECTORS
EDITIONS

• Aleister Crowley •

The Equinox Of The Gods	$150.00	10-91
Gems From The Equinox	$150.00	12-91
The Enochian World		
Of Aleister Crowley	$34.95	Now
Magick Without Tears	$79.95	Now
The Heart Of The Master	$39.95	1-92
Eight Lectures On Yoga	$39.95	11-91
The World's Tragedy	$39.95	10-91

• Christopher S. Hyatt, Ph.D. • Lon Milo DuQuette •

The Way Of The Secret Lover $34.95   Now

• Robert Anton Wilson •

Cosmic Trigger II $34.95   Now

Plus $3.50 Shipping For Each Title

NEW FALCON PUBLICATIONS
Collectors Edition Division
POB 1275
La Canada, Ca. 91012
800-882-2337

FOREWORD
TO SECOND FALCON PRINTING

Do what thou wilt shall be the whole of the Law.

Regardie received a complete copy of *The World's Tragedy* sometime in late 1982. He was very excited, so much so, that he immediately wrote an introduction and sent it to us for publication. We dropped everything and typed the manuscript into our computer. Within two months we began electronic transfer to the typesetter and started programming in the necessary type codes. Advertising began and orders began to come in. Regardie, however, became very concerned about the progress of the *The Complete Golden Dawn System of Magic*. We decided that his epic work was a more important project at the time and *The World's Tragedy* was put on the back burner. *The Complete Golden Dawn System of Magic* was completed in the fall of 1984. All were overjoyed and exhausted and the idea of producing another book was horrific.

As we saw October approaching we simply decided to celebrate and relax for the remainder of the year. When the new year appeared we promised ourselves that we would finish *The World's Tragedy* upon our return from Hawaii. Regardie planned to meet us there sometime in March. We hoped to get him settled in Hawaii and to inaugurate our plans for New Falcon Publications, the Regardie Foundation & Temple. As the fates would have it he would never make this trip—instead he underwent his Great Initiation at 7:15pm on March 10th, 1985.

In April, I returned to Sedona to settle his affairs, again delaying the republication of The World's Tragedy until October 1985.

The World's Tragedy is the indictment, just trial, conviction and execution in word and image of a religious-political system which has all but destroyed man's true nature, driving it to frustrated expressions of violence and self destruction. Crowley,

I

himself, a victim of the hoax, could not say enough in expressing his pain, disgust and contempt.

Now at a time when fundamentalist movements, both Christian and Islamic, have grown enormously in size and strength we feel it is important to republish this little masterpiece. We agree with Regardie that the force exhibited by these fanatical groups is a sign of their final death pangs. However, a terminal cancer patient can take a long time to die and during this process they are often prone to make unwise and impulsive decisions which can cause much damage to family and resources.

America, in the last ten years has seen a continuing surge in popularity within the Christian-Right of what is called **Dominion Theology.** This movement, embraced by some of the most influential leaders of the Charismatic and Evangelical denominations and governmental leaders, advocates a religious government based not on the Constitution but upon "Christian" interpretation of the "Laws of God." This includes the dictation of a State Religion and the circumscription of the Rights of nonbelievers.

The republication of *The World's Tragedy* is a timely retort to those who advocate rule by a religious dictatorship. Yet this too is a manifestation of the Divine. Even the "Devil" is His creation, something which exoteric religion will not tell the masses. God is not simply in everything, but, everything (and no-thing) is God. This esoteric view has been known from the beginning—each individual is an unique expression of the Manifestation. While the general principles remain the same, the method of expression changes, and yet through all the changes everything remains the same—an expression of the Unchangeable One. This point of view allows each man to be a "Light unto himself—since he too is the Divine" sooner or later rejoining the Infinite. This world view is in distinct contradiction to the one expressed by the fundamentalists. While we find their myopic attempts to catch God in a hair net humorous at times our primal reaction is one of horror.

For almost two thousand years history has recorded the atrocities committed in the name of the Prince of Peace. Assuming he was an historical character, Rabbi Jesus (Joshua) would be ap-Paul-led with what has been done to the ancient teachings he preached. The spirit of Christos has not been, nor can it be realized by methods and principals which inculcate fear and self-hate in the minds of children. In fact, quite the contrary has occurred, the spirit of Christos has been submerged—lost in the hysterical ranting and ravings of those who prefer the death worshipping dogma of "Cold Boiled Jesus" to the Power of Light.

The idea of a state-religion which doesn't allow personal spiritual progress is frightening. Yet even in the atrocities of Nazi Germany may be seen a purposeful expression of the Divine. However, if a fascist state-religion becomes a reality, we will simply have to endure, each in our own way, the re-emergence of the dark ages, which Crowley and many others have predicted. While hoping they are wrong we do feel they are perhaps correct. The appearance of this book again in 1991 should remind us of the present level of spiritual freedom which we currently enjoy, and that only by active involvement in safeguarding the spiritual wisdom of the ages, can we resist the forces already set in motion.

As I reflect upon the many years of joy which I shared with Regardie I am often reminded of his deep concern for the works of Crowley and the Golden Dawn. Since his death in 1985, New Falcon Publications and the Regardie Foundation have endeavored to tip the scales toward the extension of universal spiritual liberties.

Contrary to statements made by opportunistic individuals shortly after Regardie's death, he *did* consider himself a Thelemite and was especially critical of any attempts to Christianize the Golden Dawn. He was also an enthusiastic proponent of Sex Magick and was viciously critical of any who would divorce sex from spirituality. We continue to work closely with Ordo Templi Orientis (O.T.O.) in publishing the works of Aleister Crowley and have provided a platform for the most talented contemporary Thelemic authors and artists.

It is no accident that we now present this new addition of *The World's Tragedy*. The time is ripe for an additional counter-weight to be placed on the scales. While we do not believe that it will dispel the darkness overshadowing our world at this time, we do feel it will shed some light on the causes of the bleak threatening sky. If it serves no more than the posting of a bivouac (a night guard to avoid surprise attack) then we believe that Crowley and Regardie have served us well once again.

Love is the law, love under will.

Christopher S. Hyatt, Ph.D.
Lon Milo DuQuette
Los Angeles California
September 21, 1991 E.V.

Publishers Notice

This is only the second time The World's Tragedy has appeared in print since it's original debut in 1910. Despite its format as a play/poem, to our knowledge it has never been produced as a theatrical work.

1910 was also the year Crowley produced his seven Rites of Eleusis as theatrical productions at London's Caxton Hall. Despite several good reviews, the cycle of plays were performed at that time only once. Today, primarily due to the efforts of the O.T.O., public celebrations of these "Rites" are being produced world wide.

It is the hope of the Publisher that this new addition of The World's Tragedy will find its way into the hands of a courageous theatrical producer or film maker (professional or amateur) who will see the value of the work and wish to produce it as a play or film. We encourage anyone wishing to explore this possibility further to contact us.

INTRODUCTION

Before proceeding with what needs to be said about this book by Aleister Crowley, acknowledgment must first be given to the University of Texas and to Dr. Decherd Turner, Director of its Humanities Research Center, for their kind response to my request for a copy of *The World's Tragedy*. Their xeroxed copy is deeply appreciated.

John Symonds, perhaps the most malicious of biographers of famous writers, once wrote that Crowley was not a particularly good poet. Maybe! I am offering to the general public this reprint of the 1910 Paris edition of *The World's Tragedy* so that they may judge whether Symonds knew what he was talking about. For Symonds' criticisms, let me add here — I have the most profound contempt; I have expressed this at much greater and more detailed length elsewhere (See my *Legend Of Aleister Crowley*, Falcon Press, 1983).

One of the first things that Crowley set me to do after I arrived in Paris to be his secretary in the year 1928, was to make typewritten copies of this book. It was out of print and no others, beyond his own copy were available. One original and two carbon copies were made, sometime before Christmas 1928. He took the original and first carbon, and I kept the second carbon copy. This I cherished and preserved for many long years until my house in Los Angeles was broken into by some unknown zealot who selectively stole all my Crowley first editions, amongst other valuable items, including the carbon copy of this book referred to above. I missed it badly, and despite twenty years of persistent search no other copy came my way.

Then, through various grapevines, I heard that the University of Texas had a splendid collection of Crowleyana. Upon request some years ago, a bibliography of that collection was sent me. Lo and behold! they had several copies of *The World's Tragedy*. Apparently my recent request for a xerox copy was honored upon learning that I felt very strongly about all the writings of Aleister Crowley, believing that no one piece written by him, regardless of its nature, should be permitted to vanish from public scrutiny or to remain locked up in a university library. Thus they really have done mankind a great service.

The long, almost epic poem/play is one of the most bitter and vicious diatribes against Christianity that I have ever read. Especially the preface written by Crowley also. Throughout the years, whenever I contemplated the possibility of finding a copy and re-issuing this book, it occurred to me to omit altogether the preface since biographies of Crowley were now readily available. There was no need to duplicate history. There is Crowley's own autobiography *The Confessions* which he humorously called his Autohagiography. In addition there is my own *Eye In The Triangle*, (Falcon Press, 1982) which was really an answer to Symonds' wretched vilification of Crowley. It succeeded in dragging me out of a decade of literary silence and unproductivity. Susan Roberts' excellent biography *The Magician Of The Golden Dawn* must also be mentioned. (It must not be confused with Ellic Howe's hatchet job *The Magicians Of The Golden Dawn* which I reviewed critically in *Gnostica* some years ago.) These aforementioned three, apart from some few minor others, state clearly and emphatically what Crowley was about.

But when, upon receipt of the xerox copy from Texas, I reread the Preface by Crowley, the realization dawned on me that this was not under any circumstances to be omitted. It was too powerful an indictment and historical denunciation, written in his own life blood, virulently expressing his deep and abiding hatred of Christianity — from which he never really recovered. The virus was too deeply embedded in his system, no matter how valiantly he rebelled and fought against it. The hatred was too often repeated and re-emphasized not to leave any doubt that its seeds were still actively infecting him.

Perhaps the most illuminating way of regarding this is in terms of Wilhelm Reich's concept of the character armor. Basically this comprises at least two elements — the psychic armor which for convenience sake may be compared with the Freudian superego, and the muscular armor which is the sum total of all the bodily tensions of the organism. The function of the armor — whether on the psychic level or muscular level — is to repress impulses and feelings that are not morally acceptable in terms of cultural - environmental attitudes and early family training. It is also worth reflecting that this functions both on the conscious and unconscious levels. One represses with one's body as much as with one's mind.

The armor has its origins in the earliest days, even moments of childhood, babyhood and gestation. It represents the firm hand of one or more parents, or those who stand in loco parentis, who uttered the first "no" or "don't" with or without other means of emphasis. Armor is the result of using fear and terror tactics to mold infants into "proper" replications of the cultural ethos. When it becomes fully developed, it functions autonomously and absolutely, in much the same way that the inital trainers did, demanding absolute obedience. So that the repressed material has not a chance in the world to emerge; it becomes wholly incorporated into the warp and woof of the armor. (See my book, *Reich -- His Theory and Method*, Falcon Press). If the repressed material appears at all it can only be in some modified or distorted form that bears apparently little relationship to its original nature.

It might be worthwhile for the student of Crowley to study further Wilhelm Reich's *Function Of The Orgasm* in order to gain better familiarity with these notions. They will help assuredly in an enhanced understanding of Crowley and especially of this Preface to *The World's Tragedy*.

His hatred of Christianity was not a blind unreasoned prejudicial emotion. It was indelibly rooted in his own personal experience, amplified and added to by extensive study and research all throughout his adult years. The basic cause of this undying hatred revolved around the Plymouth Brethren sect founded upon and dedicated to Biblical literalism. It was the religion of his boyhood, his parents having gone to fanatical extremes to ensure that he was a "good" Christian.

His total unmitigated hatred of Christianity is therefore no mystery. It becomes intelligible to the point where anyone with some sensitivity and compassion can have much sympathy with his point of view. All that is required is to gain some familiarity with the historical antecedents of his attitude.

His family as I have said were members of this Plymouth Brethren sect. It was a religious group that developed antagonism to the Church of England and so split off, having as the main stem of their faith biblical literalism. This was their rock, and this their guide-line through the stormy seas of life. No matter how attention might be called to the innumerable contradictions of one segment of the Bible as compared with another, these people developed a profound interpretative skill enabling them to justify and rationalize their behavior and whims at any one moment in terms of a specific chapter and verse.

The home situation presented insoluble conflicts to this boy. His father, previously a Quaker, was a devout member of this sect. He loved to challenge people wherever they happened to be on basic questions of faith and their role in life. His mother was equally fanatical, though less well-informed. She played a dominant role in the development of whatever his character came to be, and in one form or another entered symbolically into all his mystical writing. He lived at first in a spiritual, social and intellectual vacuum. It left its distorting mark on him throughout his life.

All of this is described in great detail and emotion in the Preface to this book. I trust the reader will remember it forever.

The anathema that he heaped on the schoolmaster of the Plymouth Brethren school that he had to attend, is a masterpeice of invective. It is easy to imagine him almost like one of the old Biblical prophets, coming down from the mountain, and in high dudgeon and indignation, cursing the people before him. Crowley was bred on the Bible. It was practically the only book that he was permitted to read. Its language became part and parcel of the structure of his mind. It is no wonder then that his curse has all the hall-marks of the Bible, so vitriolic and damning is it in its entirety. He wrote:

"May God bite into the bones of men the pain of that hell on earth (I have prayed often) that by them it may be sowed with salt, accursed for ever! May the maiden that passes it be barren, and the pregnant woman that beholdeth it abort! May the birds of the air refuse to fly over it! May it stand as a curse, as a fear, as an hate, among men! May the wicked dwell therein! May the light of the Sun be with-held therefrom, and the light of the Moon not lighten it! May it become the home of the shells of the dead, and may the demons of the pit inhabit it! May it be accursed, accursed, accursed — accursed for ever and ever!

And still, standing as I stand in the prime of early manhood, free from all the fetters of the body and the mind, do I curse the memory thereof unto the ages."

The short section on sodomy is about the clearest confession of his own homosexuality that I have seen issue from his pen. The Bagh-i-Muattar was written, I believe, somewhat later. While this is not my cup of tea, nevertheless each man has the right to find his own way through the sexual morass that surrounds this subject in our day. That was his way.

Yet he was not altogether homosexual. Whatever meanings may attach to the term bisexuality or to Freud's clumsy but felicitous phrase "polymorphous sexual perversions of childhood," these apply without question to him (See Norman O. Brown's shattering criticism of Freud's phrase in a book Crowley would have loved *Life Against Death*.)

That was his business, however. Nonetheless, the hatred of Christianity was not entirely his personal business. It is shared especially today by multitudes of thinking men and women. And though it may appear on the surface that Fundamentalism and Evangelism and Charismatic Christianity are spreading (even the previous President of the U.S. was numbered among their ranks), nevertheless it is the belief of many that these are the agonizing death rattles of a moribund and decadent religion. If so, Crowley's writing had a lot to do with that. He was unceasing in his eloquent denunciation of the religion that spoiled his early life and with hate and guilt ruined the lives of untold legions of human beings.

Most of those who practice any form of psychotherapy will corroborate this statement readily.

One of the major characteristics of Crowley as a person was his magnificent sense of humor which bubbled and overflowed almost without cessation. For the newcomer to his manifold literary output this humor was slightly disconcerting. Even in the midst of a colloquy on philosophy or religion or mysticism a joke or two, sometimes thoroughly ribald, would disrupt the continuity of his theme. It led some critics to believe that he was merely a jokester and therefore not to be taken seriously. Never was a greater mistake made.

In this book, the dramatic personae is hysterical by itself. Jehovah, the testy old senior of the Old Testament, is depicted as a mangy old Vulture named Yaugh Waugh. And his only begotten son "the lamb that taketh away the sins of the world," is depicted simply as the Lamb. The Holy Ghost, pictorialized by the descent of the dove, is engaged with Yaugh Waugh in machinations and plottings that do not please the Lamb in any way, and is simply named Pigeon. Their appearances on stage as it were intersperse the activities of handsome Greek lads and lassies who seem to be enjoying themselves in the dells and groves of the woodlands, quite unaware of the machinations of the unholy Three.

Let me close this short Introduction with the firm conviction that the book needs no defense. It stands on its own artistic and iconoclastic merit, which is considerable. And I must add that it gives me enormous pleasure and profound satisfaction to know that I have had a part in giving back to the world a document that is as important in its own way as the Bill of Rights is to Americans.

Israel Regardie
Arizona
1983

PREFACE

I have it on hearsay that I was born on the 12th of October in the year 1875 of Pseudo Christ. I was born dumb; and the first incident of my career was the cutting of my fraenum linguae, that I might speak plainly. The operation, as this volume shows, was a complete success. Of my early life I remember little; chiefly a large garden with, at the end of it, a wood which overlooked the road and afforded vantage for archers. There was a war in the land; my cousin Gregor Grant, six years older than myself, and a few other stern exiles, desperately banded against the rest of the neighbourhood. I remember leaping from the top of a sand pit in the character of Sir Garnet Wolseley and nearly transfixing with my father's alpenstock an astonished navvy who had not properly prepared the trying role of Arabi Pasha, suddenly and without warning assigned to him by our Army Council. I remember too being disarmed and chased by a small Italian boy (the McCallum Mohr) whose bandbox, containing doubtless an exquisite bonnet, I as Greumoch Dhuibh McAlpin had pierced with that same knotty lance. Nor shall I easily forget how we filled the tea-urn at the Brethrens' tea-fight with old Mr. Sherrall's castor-oil, to the discomfiture of the faithful, who were too polite to call the attention of the hostess to their interior pangs.

Joyful too was the great tea at Mr. Nunnerley's where we delayed the prayer meeting one whole hour by plying Mrs. Musty with avalanches of food after everyone else had finished. Ah Joy! as piglike she munched on! while the hapless brethren (torn between impatience and politeness) wrung their hands in anguish.

Only my natural reluctance to strike a tragic chord so early in my narrative obliges me to omit some account of the circumstances in which the well-named Mrs. Clapham, the fishmonger's wife, was expelled from "fellowship."

But above all I remember how we soused Leggett's boy, known as the Living Mushroom from the shape of his hat, in old Ailes's pig-tub.

And then my father died, and the note changes. To explain, I find myself obliged to give a short account of the Plymouth Brethren, their tenets, character, and history.

THE PLYMOUTH BRETHREN

The religious movement which obtained this name through the sudden and enormous success of an evangelistic crusade at Plymouth in its early days was started in Ireland.

It was an aristocratic and intellectual movement. John Nellson Darby, a learned man of good family, reasoned thus:

The Bible is the Word of God.

If its literal interpretation is once abandoned, the whole structure crashes to earth.

This it will be seen is identically the Catholic position, save that for "literal" Rome reads "Ecclesiastical." Darby, too, found himself forced into the practical admission that "literal" meant Darbeian; for some of the more obvious contradictions and absurdities in the Bible are too necessary to the practical side of religion to be ignored.

Seeing this, they devised an elaborate system of mental water-tight compartments. The contradictions of Old and New Testament were solved by a Doctrine that what was sauce for the Jewish "Dispensation" was not necessarily sauce for the Christian "Dispensation." Cleverer than Luther, they made possible the Epistle of James by a series of sophisms which really deserve to be exposed as masterpieces of human self-deception. My space forbids.

So, despite all the simplicity of the original logical position, they were found shifting as best they might from compromise to compromise. But this they never saw themselves; and so far did they take their principle that my father would refuse to buy railway shares because railways were not mentioned in the Bible! Of course the practice of finding a text everything means ultimately "I will do as I like," and I suspect my father's heroics only meant that he thought a slump was coming.

Their attitude to human reason, too, was simply wonderful.

Some Wicked Man would point out that the Jonah story was contrary to our experience of possibility.

The P.B. — The word is not "whale" in the Hebrew: it probably means "dog-shark."

(This "solution" is actually printed in a book of the liar and slanderer Torrey).

THE W.M. — Our experience of dog-sharks tells us —

THE P.B. — What, after all is human reason? To the Greeks foolishness, etc. The wisdom of man is foolishness, etc. We must have faith.

THE W.M. — In men?

THE P.B. — Never. In God!

THE W.M. — But you believe in the Bible?

THE P.B. — Every word of it, thank God!

THE W.M. — In the Protestant or the Catholic Bible? The Bible was written by men, translated by men, criticised by scholars again and again. You accept all the criticisms up to 1611 and reject all later. Why?

THE P.B. — There is a place prepared for the devil and his angels to which you (my poor dear brother) will most surely go! Why not simply accept Christ as your Saviour and Lord? (Then he gets started; and the rest must be heard to be believed).

So — is it a type of all logic? — their simple Yea and Nay became more casuistical than Dens or Escobar, and their strict adhesion to the Commands of the bible became a mere loosening of the strings of conscience.

An irreligious man may have moral checks; a Plymouth Brother has none. He is always ready to excuse the vilest crimes by quoting the appropriate text, and invoking the name of Christ to cover every meanness which may delight his vain and vicious nature.

For the Plymouth Brethren were in themselves an exceptionally detestable crew. The aristocrats who began the movement were of course just aristocrats, and their curious system left them so. But they ran a form of "Early Christian" Spiritual Socialism, by having no appointed priest or minister, and they were foolish enough to favour their followers financially.

Thus Mr. Giblets — let us call him — the third-best butcher in the village found (on the one hand) that while at church he was nobody at all, and in the chapel an elder, in the little meeting in the Squire's morning-room he was no less than the minister of God and the mouthpiece of the Holy Ghost; just as on the other hand it was only natural that the orders from the Hall should come his way, and leave the first-best butcher lamenting, and the second-best bewildered. So that in my time the sect (though it is only fair to point out that they refused to be described as a sect, since what they had done was not to form a new sect, but to "come out of sect", — this they maintained in spite of the fact that they were far more exclusive than any other religious body in Europe) was composed of a few of the old guard, my father the last of them all, and the meanest crew of *canaille* that ever wriggled.

With my father's death the small schims which had hitherto lopped off a few members every year or two were altogther surprassed by the great Raven heresy which split the body into two equal halves, and extinguished the last sparks of its importance.

I am going beyond my subject, but I cannot refrain from telling the awful story of the Meeting at Oban.

The Meeting at Oban consisted of a Mr. Cameron and his wife and the bedridden mother of one of the two. I forget which. Now as it is written: "wheresoever two or three are gathered together in my name, there am I in the midst of them" it was all very well: but two forms a quorum. Jesus will not come for less. This has never been disputed by any doctor of the Brethren. Wigram is clean on the point; if Darby had ever been clear on any point, it would have been on that; Kelly never denied it; even Stuart was sound in this matter, and Stoney himself (though reluctantly) gave his adhesion. To hold a Meeting you must have two persons present. Let nobody try to upset this; for once I positively insist. No less than two for a Meeting! I will brook no opposition; I mean to have my own way in the matter; I am not to be played with. Two or more make a Meeting. There; my foot is down, let's hear no more senseless cavil about it!

Well, I need hardly say that Mr. and Mrs. Cameron took opposite sides of the controversy. When the glad wires flashed the message that Mr. Raven in the Meeting at Ealing had deliberately said with slow and weighty emphasis: "He that hath the Son hath eternal life". Mrs. Cameron almost wept for joy. When (the message continued) Major Mc. Arthy had risen to his feet and retorted: "He that hath the Son of God hath everlasting life", Mr. Cameron executed a Highland though funereal fling.

When Mr. Raven, stung to the quick, had shaken his fist at the Major and yelled: "Brother, you're a sinful old man! Mrs. Cameron "had always known there was something" and invented a ruined governess. But — oh the laughter of her husband when the telegraph brought the Major's retort: "Brother, have you no sin?" Spoken with an accent of mildness which belied the purple of his face.

In short, the Meeting at Oban had split. Mr. Cameron had withdrawn from the Lord's supper!!! It was therefore absolutely necessary for both of them to assure themselves that the bedridden mother was of their way of thinking, or neither could hold the "Morning Meeting"; though I suppose either could preach the Gospel — morosa voluptas!

Unhappily, that excellent lady was a hard case. She was quite deaf and very nearly blind; while mentally she had never been remarkable for anything beyond a not unamiable imbecility. However, there was but one thing to be done, to argue her into conviction.

They agreed to take eight-hour shifts; and for all I know, they are arguing still, and neither of the Meetings at Oban can meet!

A BOYHOOD IN HELL

The Revd. H. d'Arcy Champney M.A. of Corpus Christi College, Cambridge, had come out of sect.

He had voted at the Parliamentary elections by crossing out the names of the candidates and writing: "I vote for King Jesus".

He had started a school for the Sons of Brethren at 51, Bateman Street, Cambridge. May God bite into the bones of men the pain of that hell on earth (I have prayed often) that by them it may be sowed with salt, accursed for ever! May the maiden that passes it be barren, and the pregnant woman that beholdeth it abort! May the birds of the air refuse to fly over it! May it stand as a curse, as a fear, as an hate, among men! May the wicked dwell therein! May the light of the Sun be withheld therefrom, and the light of the Moon not lighten it! May it become the home of the shells of the dead, and may the demons of the pit inhabit it! May it be accursed, accursed, accursed — accursed for ever and ever!

And still, standing as I stand in the prime of early manhood, free from all the fetters of the body and the mind, do I curse the memory thereof unto the ages.

It was a good enough school from the point of examiners, I daresay. Morally and physically it was an engine of destruction and corruption. I am just going to put down a few facts haphazard as they come to my memory; you may form you own judgment.

1. We were allowed to play Cricket, but not to score runs, lest it should excite the vice of "emulation".

2. Champney told me, a child of not yet twelve years old, that he had never consummated his marriage, (Only the very acute verbal memory which I possess enabled me years after to recall and interpret his meaning. He used a coarser phrase).

3. We were told that "the Lord had a special care of the school, and brought to light that which was done in darkness", etc., etc., *ad nauseam*. "The instrument was on this occasion so-and-so, who had nobly come forward, etc., etc". In other words, hypocrisy and sneaking were the only virtues.

Naturally, one of several boys who might be involved in the same offence would take fright and save his skin by sneaking. The informer was always believed implicitly, as against probability, or even possiblity, with complete disregard of the testimony of other and independent witnesses.

For instance, a boy named Glascott, with insane taint, told Mr. Champney that he had visited me (12 years old) at my mother's house during the holidays — true so far, he had — and found me lying drunk at the bottom of the stairs". My mother was never asked about this; nor was I told of it. I was put into "Coventry" i.e. nor master nor boy might speak to me, or I to them. I was fed on bread and water; during playhours I worked in the school room;

during work hours I walked solitary round and round the playground. I was expected to "confess" the crime of which I was not only innocent, but unaccused.

This punishment, which I believe criminal authorities would considere severe on a prisoner, went on for a term and a half. I was, at last, threatened with expulsion for my refusal to "confess", and so dreadful a picture of the horrors of expulsion did they paint me — the guilty wretch, shunned by his fellows, slinks on through life to a dishonoured grave, etc. — that I actually chose to endure my torture, and to thank my oppresor.

Physically, I broke down. The strain and the misery affected my kidneys; and I had to leave school altogether for two years. I should add in fairness that there were other accusations against me, though, as you shall hear, were almost equally silly.

I learnt at last, through the intervention of my uncle, in a lucid interval, what I was supposed to have done. I was said to have tried "to corrupt Chamberlain" — not our great patriotic statesman, shifty Joe — but a boy. (I was 12 years old, and quite ignorant of all (sexual matters till long after). Also I had "held a mock prayer meeting". This I remembered. I had strolled up to a group of boys in the playground, who were indeed holding one. As they saw me one said: "Brother Crowley will now lead us in prayer". Brother Crowley was too wary, and walked away. But instead of doing what a wise boy would have done: gone straight to the head, and accused them of forty-six distinct unmentionable crimes, I let things slide. So, fearing that I might go, the hurried off themselves, and told him how that wicked Crowley had tried to lead them away from Jesus.

Worse, I had called Page 1 a Pharisee. That was true; I had said it. Dreadful of me! And Page 1, who "walked very close to Jesus", of course went and told.

Yes, they all walked close to Jesus — as close as Judas did.

4. A boy named Barton was sentenced to 120 strokes of the cane on his bare shoulders, for some petty theft of which he was presumably innocent.

Superb was the process of trial. It began by an extra long prayer-time, and Joshua's account of the sin of Achan, impressively read. Next, an hour or two about the Lord's care of the school, the way He brought sin to light. Next, when well worked up, and all our nerves on the jump, who stole what? Silence. Next, The Lord's care in providing a witness — like the witnesses against Naboth! Then the witness and his story, as smooth as a policeman's. Next, sentence. Last, execution, with intervals of prayer!

Champney's physique being impaired, one may suppose by his excessive devotion to Jesus, he arranged to give 60 strokes one day, and 60 the next.

My memory fails — perhaps Barton will one day oblige with his reminiscenses — but I fancy the first day come so near killing him that he escaped the second.

I remember one licking I got — on the legs, because flogging the buttocks excites the victim's sensuality! — 15 minutes prayer, 15 more strokes of the cane — and more prayer to top it!

5. On Sunday the day was devoted to "religion". Morning prayers and sermon (about 45 min.). Morning "Meeting" (1½ to 2 hours). Open-air preaching on Parker's Piece (say 1 hour). Bible reading and learning by heart. Reading of the few books "sanctioned for Sunday" (say 2 hours). Prayer-meeting (called voluntary, but to stay away meant that some sneak in the school would accuse you of something next day), (say 1 hour). Evening prayer and Sermon (say 30 minutes). Preaching of the Gospel in the meeting-room (1½ hours). Ditto on Parker's Piece (say 1 hour). Prayer before retiring (say ½ hour).

6. The "Badgers' Meeting". Every Monday night the school was ranged round the back of the big schoolroom, and the scourings of Barnswell (Cambridge's slum) let in, fed, preached to, and dismissed.

Result, epidemics of ring worms, measles, and mumps.

Oh no! not a result; the Lord's hand was heavy upon us because of some undiscovered sin.

I might go on for a long while, but I will not. I hope there are some people in the world happy enough to think that I am lying, or a least exaggerating. But I pledge my word to the literal truth of all I have said, and there are plenty of witnesses alive to confirm me, or to refute me. I have given throughout the actual names, addresses and other details.

ADOLESCENCE

Too ill with albuminuria brought on by the savage treatment of Champney to do any regular work, I was sent away with various tutors, mostly young men from Cambridge, members of the unspeakable C.I.C.C.U.

I remember in my first term at Cambridge how I was in the rooms of a leading light of the C.I.C.C.U., the Revd. Something Doddridge, my Uncle Tom's trusted henchman.

I remember how eloquently he held forth on the courage to stop any "impure conversation". I remember how impressed we were; how a gentleman with an "honourable" in front of his name, destined to be celebrated in the world of motors and balloons, walked into the room and told us rather a lively story. The Reverend Something Doddridge thought of the "honourable" and laughed pleasantly.

I remember how, boys as we were, we filed austerely from the rooms without farewell. Oh, you must know the C.I.C.C.U.!

I remember too how this Doddridge, while in charge of my morals, aided and abetted me in extinguishing street lamps; and how when a policeman pounced upon me, he forsook me and fled! A true disciple of Jesus!

I had no playmates; my morals might be corrupted! Only the "children of brethren" were eligible, and these were as a rule socially impossible.

I was always being watched for signs of masturbation, and always being warned and worried about it. It says something for human innocence that after four years of this insane treatment I was still absolutely ignorant, though on fire in every nerve to learn the practice that people made so much fuss about.

But really — my tutors! Of all the surpassing prigs! I was so mentally shattered by the disease and torture — for both continued — that I remember practically nothing of the next two years.

But at least I shall take care that this book comes into the hands of the Very Reverend Armitage Robinson Esq., M.A., D.D., Dean of Westminster; for though I suppose he knows how his missionary brother Jack seduced to sodomy his missionary brother Fred, he may still be ignorant of how that brother Fred (one of my tutors) attempted to seduce me in his own mother's house at Maze Hill. This came a little later; and I knew exactly what he was doing, as it happened. I let him go as far as he did, with the deliberate intention of making sure on that point.

I think my readers will agree — enough of my tutors!

I ought to make an honourable exception of one Archibald Douglas, an Oxford man and a traveller. He taught me sense and manhood, and I shall not easily forget my debt to him. I hear he is dead — may earth lie light upon him!

Of course my Mother and her brother my uncle Tom couldn't stand him. (I must excuse my mother and my Uncle. The former was the best of all possible mothers, only marred beyond belief by the religious monomania which perhaps started in what one may call "Hysteria of Widowhood"; the later a typical sexual degenerate.) They stole his letters and faked up some excuse for getting rid of him. And if "an orphan's curse can drag to hell a spirit from on high" what of the curse of a child on those who betrayed him in their bigotry and meanness to such torture as I have described?

My whole soul cramped; society denied me; books debarred me, with the rare exceptions of Scott, Ballantyne, and some of Dickens, with a few even worse!

To illustrate the domestic principles of literary criticism:

I was forbidden David Copperfield because of "little Em'ly" — Emily being my Mother's name, I might cease to respect her. For the same reason she proscribed the Bab Ballads, recommended by a rash tutor, because "Emily Jane was a nursery maid!" Coleridge's Ancient Mariner was condemned because of the water-snakes whom he "blessed unaware"; snakes being cursed in Genesis!

As it happened, however, I had a backbone in me some where. I had always refused to join the sneaking hypocrite gang at Champney's; now I accepted the war, and began to fight for my freedom. I went on long walks in the mountains, where my tutors could not follow me, and where delightful peasant girls could and did follow me — God bless them!

One day I had a difference of opinion with a tutor, in the course of which he fell from a rock into a loch (whose name I forgot) near Forsinard. Memory fails to recall the actual cause of dispute; but I think I had thrown his fishing-rod into the loch, and thought that it was expedient for him to try and retrieve it.

The same night he found me in the heather with Belle McKay the local beauty (God bless her!), and gave me up as a bad job.

So I fought the swine! They sent me to Malvern, where my weakness made me the prey of every bully, and saved me from the attention of every budding Eulenburg. Sodomy was the rule at Malvern; my study-companion used even to take money for it. I cunningly used my knowledge of the fact to get taken away from the school.

It must not be supposed that we had no other amusements. There was "pill-ragging"; a form of fight whose object was to seize and hurt the opponent's testicles; and "greasing"; i.e., spitting either in each other's faces or secretly so the victim should not detect the act. In my time this had died out of the other houses; but still flourished in my house "Huntingdon's" N 4. There was bullying, too; and now and then cricket and football.

They sent me to Tonbridge; my health broke down; partly, one may say, through what would have been my own fault or misfortune if I had been properly educated; but, as it was, was the direct result of the vile system that, not content with torturing me itself, handed me over bound and blindfold to the outraged majesty of Nature. I escaped then from Tonbridge. They sent me to Eastbourne to a P.B. family where I had more liberty, and could have been happy; but the revolting cruelties which they inflicted on the only pretty and decent member of the family, my dear "sister" Isabelle, caused me one day to knock their heads together and walk out of the house. They sent me to Cambridge. I found myself my own master, and settled down to lead a righteous, sober and godly life; and to make up for lost time in the matter of education.

Outside purely scholastic subjects, they had taught me to fight, to love the truth, to hate oppression, — and by God! I think they taught me well.

On my soul, I should thank them!

THE WRITING OF THE WORLD'S TRAGEDY

It has been necessary to sketch this part of my life in order to exhibit the atmosphere which I am bound to connect with Christianity, or at least English Christianity.

Certainly the vast majority of English people, of those who are religious at all, belong either to Evangelicalism or Dissent; and the tyranny of these is nearly if not quite as bad as that of the Plymouth Brethren. I had, however, cut myself adrift from all these things. I had lived among the great men of the earth, and the great mountains of the earth. Pollitt had made a poet of me; Eckenstein had made a man of me; Cecil Jones and Allan Bennett had made a God of me. I had forgotten the Plymouth Brethren! But early in this spring, I went down to Eastbourne to my mother's house, and some of the old bitterness came back. In her house were two vile old women, hypocrites and slaves to the marrow. The mere meanness and old maid-ishness of it would have sickened me. These mange-bitten cats!

But there was worse. Only one food was on the table for breakfast, lunch, and dinner; and that food cold boiled Jesus. I stomached it well enough — God's blood! I had my belly full of yore and knew to despise it — but in vain I tried to talk of other things. The Boulter blasphemy case was on, and the cold boiled Jesus was so high that it literally stank. So did the women! I stood it for breakfast, I stood it for lunch, I stood it for tea — but 'twasn't tea,'twas Jesus!

Dinner came; cold boiled Jesus, and the scrag end of it at that!

I went out and stood by the sea. I was lost in reverie. Here were these hags of hell, the product of an unvarying diet of cold boiled Jesus! By God! Could not I save somebody? These had once been fresh healthy English girls, fit for life and laughter. C.B.J. had mummified them to what they were. I would be the Saviour of the future!

I must have wandered in my meditation; for presently I found myself lying on the grass under the full moon and the stars, the sea's low plash beneath my feet, the soft breeze blowing over me, a whisper — oh essence of the winds and of the seas of the world! — in my ears (I seem to remember even now that her name was

Mabel — thank you, Mabel!) and then I gazed upon the moon and vowed myself knight Artemis, to bring the truth into this England of hypocrisy, light in its superstition of rationalism, love in its prudery, chastity into its whoredom!

So I swore, and rose up and kissed Mabel and went home in the might of the holy vision — for the god Pan appeared to me, and abode in me and I in him — and wrote for four nights — night by night, until the World's Tragedy lay finished and perfect before me.

All day I kept myself up to the mark by the stern penance of C.B.J.; all night I wrote — and wrote.

So fierce I wrote that — six months later — I have written no word since. I have pored forth all the vials, and loosed all the seals. From that supreme effort I am fallen exhausted — until, as it may chance, the Gods renew my vigour. And all my other work I count as nothing; for I have written this in Pan, and in Pan I am content. To the boys and girls of England I give my book, the charter of their freedom.

ALICE WESLEY TORR OR ALEISTER CROWLEY?

With one thing and another to worry me I was a nervous wreck all this March and April of 1908. I was wasting my time in constructing anagrams of my name to publish this book under. Which shows how dependant the best of us is on his in'ards. If an Army marches on its belly, so does a philosopher think on his. My best on another's.

So lost indeed was I in this jungle of delusion that I was quite surprised when one beautiful sunset in May, sitting at ease under the shadow of the Lion de Belfort, I became aware of a temptation of the devil. Quite a number of people had been asking me during the last few months to compromise with respectability. And by Jove! I nearly did! I was ill — forgive the wavering! I am wise in time, luckily, and my "Retro Satanas" takes this form.

Let me define my position. It is quite true that my attitude to real life, the life of Nature, is perfectly "sane" and "wholesome." In a perfect society I should regard even my "Alice" as perverted art: for in a sane world one is insane to proclaim insanity. But art (which is the Word of the Masters to the World) must move with that world and follow it into its corruption, redeeming the same. The simple humanity, the great guffawing indecency, of Shakespeare is well enough for the pagan society of Elizabeth. The splendid savage Jehovah is sane enough and grand enough for nomadic Israel. But since then the World is Christianized, and there is a need for the bitterness of Shelley and Byron, the intense "justification by sin" doctrine of Swinburne. Perhaps we are wrong to have thought of Swinburne as having recanted; it may be that he said to himself; "Well, I'm sick of these dogs! I will write simple lyrics and shut out the world." Still, the result is not good. Moreover we who are in the forefront of the fight are annoyed with Achilles — and anyhow there is no excuse for such a Patroclus as Watts-Dunton!

Well, however that may be, here we are in the fight; and if I am called an anarchist, soit! But I throw my bomb with a difference. If I do not throw a physical bomb, it is only because there is none big enough. For the Government is in the hands of the bourgoisie and the canaille, and it is for us aristocrats to throw the bombs. There can be no peace between Socrates and Athens, between Jesus and Jerusalem. We must then first throw moral bombs, and this book is mine!

It is a curious position. All my sympathy is with my own class — birth, education, wealth, courage, pride. These are my heritage. But all my own people are busy pretending to love the dirty, stinking, lousy, poor; Coriolanus "licking the breech of a leprous hangman." (Not Crowley, this time: Catullus).

So that on mature consideration I drop the Revd. C. Verey of "Clouds without Water" — it is only one more satire. The invention was not cowardice but art. My sympathies are entirely with the alleged author of the Quatorzains; in a world of Winnington-Ingrams it is about the best that any one can do.

At the same time, I have a foible: I should like to produce ideal poetry; poetry free from the false conditions of modern crapulence. "Clouds without Water" and this World's Tragedy are mostly nonsense to a Nina Oliver or a Dorothy Lamb, those avatars of Pagan art. But to a Dilke, lamed by a kick from the British ass; or to a Burton, swimming in the Sea of Glue — they must seem miracles of virility and truth. Natural love and love of Nature are poetry everywhere; and (idleness!) I hope one day to be able to leave the English hypocrites to their own beastliness, and live in my own world. Until I am wanted; in the hour of battle. One thing I must ask; let this book be assiduously circulated among the young. There is hope there if anywhere. Let me seduce the boys of England, and the oldsters may totter unconverted to their graves. Then these boys, becoming men, may bring about the new heaven and the new earth. You are not a Crowleian till you can say fervently "Yes, thank God, I am an atheist." For the 'transvaluation of all values' must yet again take place, when those are all dead and damned who have forced us into the painful position we now occupy.

The "man-eating beasts because of whom we dare not love thee," once gone, we can revive the true cultus of the Logos; the chastity mongering masturbators once swept away, we can without reproach follow our natural inclination to purity: the lawyers and millionnaires and demagogues once squelched, we can enjoy our property without alarm.

Young men! there is the enemy. I am no coward, I hope; and believe that I may make a fairly good general — at least no traitor. But without an army I am useless; a Napoleon at St. Helena.

Give me my army, young men; and we will sweep these dogs into the sea. Those in the front rank will have the honour of getting killed first.

PORNOGRAPHY

Now to give battle one must find a disputed point, and struggle for its mastery. English pudibundery being the main strong hold of the Puritan, I now concentrate my guns on that position.

With the exception of the Chinese classics and one or two of the Hindu and Buddhist, all authors of antiquity are wholly or partially concerned to discourse frankly, joyously, amusingly, of the sexual act. Of modern authors we observe that only the pornographic survive. Shakespeare, Sterne, Swift, Rabelais, Villon, — what names have we to put against these? Milton and some lesser.

And to-day? What authors of the last century do we find on our shelves? Byron, exiled, yet with wealth sufficient to mock his foes; Shelley, expelled from Oxford, exiled, robbed of his children; Keats, bullied into consumption; Blake, nigh starved; Flaubert, Baudelaire, Gautier, Zola, Richepin all prosecuted, suppressed; Verlain, his life a mere holiday between spells of prison. I cannot quote you the good authors, the popular authors; neither I nor any one else can remember their names.

All this babble about indecency is the merest froth; as Vizetelly dies, broken by imprisonment for the crime of having translated Zola, the same Zola is being feasted at the Guildhall by the Lord Mayor of London.

But, then, of course, the question arises "what is pornography?"

It has been justly remarked that the greatest men are those who play upon the whole scale of human emotions, from the spiritual to the obscene. The humour of Aristophanes, Shakespeare, Sterne, and Rabelais is identical with that of the ordinary smoking-room story; only a deal better done. Nor is there any other eternal humour; other kinds depend on the accidents of the age.

You never find a single impure line in any of these authors, any gloating on impurity. The laughter is hearty, there is no schoolboy sniggering — no consciousness of guilt.

(So even with Keats' Gadfly and Sharing Eve's Apple; Browning's bawdy jests in Pippa Passes, the Ring and the Book, One Word More, La Saisiaz and elsewhere; cleaner, truly, than the furtive eroticism in Prometheus Unbound. Shelley was more consciously under the curse of Jesus.) It is this "consciousness of sin" which is to my mind the essentially Christian attitude. It is this which inspires the outcry against art and simple pleasures: these swine nose everwhere for filth, and grunt with shocked glee when they find it.

All serious subjects are tabooed as "bad form!" (I must add in parenthesis that the eugenic prigs and sex-problem pigs are every whit as bad. They are just as shocked at Rabelais as the other Puritans).

There is nothing impure in passion, if only it be elemental and strong. The whole soul storms the height of heaven, exults, laughs, enjoys, falls exhausted. The thing is clean.

It is the lady novelist that drags her snail-track across the desert of bad literature. Nothing so excites my loathing as to see these ghouls licking their chops over the adventures of some dirty slut of a Princess. They scent indecency in passion beyond the marriage-tie: they will not even allow a man to be in love with his own wife. Why shouldn't he be? He is now and then. I happen to know it. The long and short of the whole matter is this, that there is nothing clean but ecstasy.

Whether that ecstasy is the divine spirituality of Visvarupad-arshana, or the sexual splendour of Epipsychidion, or the laughter of Catullus, all is pure and perfect.

It is the vision of the God that is pure; it is the veils that stain. Whether the curtain of falsehood be moral, or ethical, or romantic, it is a stain, Weakness is evil and impure; strength is divine and clean.

A mountain is more naked than a marsh. By your leave, gentles, I will continue to live on the mountain.

SODOMY

Further, lest 'broad-minded' prigs come to smash me by their aid, I shall fight openly for that which no living Englishman dare defend, even in secret — sodomy!

At school I was taught to admire Plato and Aristotle, who recommend sodomy to youths. I am not so rebellious as to oppose their dictum; and in truth there seems no better way to avoid the contamination of woman and the morose pleasures of solitary vice. (Not that women themselves are unclean. It is the worship of them as ideals that rots the soul). Again we may say that all the great men of antiquity were sodomites: Socrates, Caesar, Alexander, Martial, Catullus, Virgil, Achilles; Napoleon, Frederick the Great, Goethe, Shakespeare, Bacon, an unbroken line of English monarchs; Mohammed, Benvenuto Cellini, Wilde, Symonds, Emerson, Pater, Fitz-Gerald, Leighton, Whitman, Michael Angelo, Leonardo, and a host of others — even unto this hour. But of this hour I will not speak. I am now collecting a great body of evidence similar to that which Herr Harden has gathered in Germany, and involving an even higher class of society. Not in the least to show the corruptions of that class; but to proclaim sodomy as an aristocratic virtue, which our middle class had better imitate if they wish to be smart.

If I have not already published the correspondence in the possession between the late Duke of Clarence and Boy Morgan — as well as many other important papers — and a pretty penny they have cost me! — it is not for any dog-in-the manger reasons, but because it would coincide so dramatically with the moment when, like Socrates, I get into trouble for corrupting morality, and because I never like to leave a job half done. It is almost incredible how large a number of peers there are against whom I have not a shadow of evidence or even suspicion. Luckily the judges are less wary. While the bishops are such easy game as to be hardly worth powder and shot.

There, I've done it now! *Vous avez ecrit contre le bon Dieu; c'est mauvais, mais Il le vous pardonnera. Vous avez ecrit contre Jesus-Christ; c'est pire encore, mais Il le vous pardonnera. Mais vous avez ecrit Leurs Excellences, et Elles ne le vous pardonneront jamais.*

But this lion can bite back!

Nor after all, is fear precisely the sentiment inspired by the spectacle of a nation which has so recently placed at the head of its affairs that William Ewart Gladstone who shaped his policy by the predictions of a charlatan clairvoyant in Bond Street, while his drunken harlot performed her watery exploits on the stage of Drury Lane Theatre.

The proofs, too, (in my hands) that a certain member of the present Cabinet derives much of his income from the profits of a brothel, lend a certain solidity to my position.

This lion can bite back.

CHRISTIANITY

But why — we may indeed ask — all this heavy metal to bombard a brothel? Has no good thing come out of Nazareth?

It is in a way extremely trying to live in a world where connotation varies so wildly.

The Sicilian peasant who can roar with laughter at some blasphemous obscenity of his village priest while preserving his devotion to the deities satirized, will justly be astonished and disgusted with me. He will hardly credit that anyone can take deities so seriously as to do anyone an injury on their behalf. He is at heart a Pagan; Mary is his mistress and Jesus his -- Bambino --, and he loves to play with them in the woods where the sunlight traces its faint fan-patterns among the leaves.

The idea of a Jesus who objected to people playing on a Sunday — who insisted on being worshipped in a silk hat and frock coat, who couldn't stand people obtaining refreshment after 12:30 — Well, it never struck him, that's all!

So when I go wandering among country-side Catholics I am nearly as happy in their simple worship as I am with the grander and austerer conceptions of Mohammed. But England! The people have materialized their God into a Parish Councillor, at the best; at the worst, he has been made the excuse of every crime.

The prevalence of syphilis in the Indian army has increased from 8% to 80% lest God should be shocked by our unholy recognition of the human nature of the human soldier.

It is useless to multiply examples. All I wish to do is to justify my agreement with Shelly and Nietzsche in defining Christianity as the religious expression of the slave spirit in man.

I do not wish to argue that the doctrines of Jesus, they and they alone, have degraded the world to its present condition. I take it that Christianity is not only the cause but the symptom of slavery. There were slaves in Rome, of course, even under the republic. But it was only through Paul that the slime found tongue, and uttered its agony and blasphemy. Now, through the steady growth of altruism pari-passu with the Gospel that advocates it, the world is come to such a pass that the canaille is throned.

The Old Age Pensions folly, which is simply the offical seal upon the survival of the unfittest, a check to honest ambition, a playing into the hands of the unskillful and the vicious, of all those (in short) whom a healthy organism crushes as the first condition of its well-being, is so "popular" that of all the House of Commons, the majority of whom see as plainly as I do how things stand, barely 1% are found to oppose it root and branch, and they from constituencies which the act will hardly touch, while the Lords — our bulwark, oh God! and what a fortress is that whose semi-lunes are Lord Townshend and Lord Tankerville! — pass the bill with scarce a protest. We are to be taxed beyond endurance, our defences neglected, our education left to sink or swim as it may, that our whole state may be clogged with its own excrement! It is no idle boast of the vermin Socialists that their system is Christianity, and no other is genuine. And look at them! To a man — or rather to a Tetragrammaton which is a Temurah of T.H.I.S. — they are atheists and in favour of Free Love — whatever that may mean. I have talked with many Socialists, but never with one who understood his subject. Empty babblers they are, muddle-headed philanthropists. They read a shilling abridgement of John Stuart Mill, and settle all economic problems over a -- sirloin of turnips -- in some filthy crank food dive. Ask them any simple question about detail, and the bubble is pricked.

Well, as I was saying, they are all in favour of -- Free Love --. Some paper mentioned the fact. What a stampede! Oh no! Not me, please sire, it was the other boy. It would never do to shock the British public.

If I exclude Bernard Shaw and H.G. Wells from these strictures, it is because Shaw is simply a masturbating monkey, and Wells a satirist playing at castles on his Sandgate sands. So, then, it is Christianity considered as slavishness, as fear of all sorts, as altruism — that exquisite refinement of fear which we call sympathy — that I condemn. It is because we are afraid of death that the death of others affects us, except of course in the case of bereavement.

Just look at your Christian when he gets his modicum of manhood. He will not take the manly way, because (a) he is afraid of hurting the modesty of the poor girl (who is simply aching for him); (b) he is afraid of catching some disease; (c) he might get her into trouble; (d) what will the neighbours say?; (e) suppose she said no, what a fool I should look!; (f) God said I mustn't. And so on through the alphabet of cowardice.

Look at your Christian as he sits down to dinner.

He won't eat melon because the weather is hot, and he might get cholera; mutton? Think of the poor sheep! Potatoes? Bad for his fat; Artichoke? Bad for his gout. Tomatoes? Cause of cancer. Wine? The great curse of our day, my dear sir. Milk? A mere mass of tubercle bacilli. Water? Typhoid! Do you want to poison me, my dear friend? Beer? Well, perhaps a little beer — for he has shares in a brewery.

You have already seen how this awful fear of nature and of God is twisted into an engine of oppression and torture against any one who declines to grovel and cringe before their filthy fetish. It is obvious that cowardice is the cause of cruelty: the brave man strikes a strenuous blow, and all is over; the coward brought to bay snarls and strikes in desperation, and if by chance the blow goes home, he jumps on and mutilates and insults his victim.

Of course all this insane Christianity has produced its own toxin. Our prudery goes hand in hand with the most disgusting system of prostitution in the world, and our Theatres (too pure for that corrupter Sophocles) are disgraced by the most senseless and witless legshows. Our praise of poverty has produced the worst poor-laws in civilization; our democracy has perfected a snobbery which would make Thackeray stare with surprise. Queen Victoria the Good — what a washerwoman lost to mankind! was the French nation's epitaph upon her — drove the last nail into the coffin of art in England. Though 'twas needless cruelty: whom have we had of the first rank in England since Elizabeth but the Revolutionaries? Blake, Shelley, Keats, Coleridge, Byron, Swinburne, Swift, Butler, Milton, every one exiled, starved, bullied, driven insane; except Milton, whose supreme hypocrisy saved him, as it damned the nation forever. Anyhow, bad as it was, Victoria made it worse, and, under a queen with a high-necked collar, it is left for me to unite in myself all the blare of all the trumpets. Call me Israfel, last of the angels, and let the dead rise from their tombs!

I therefore hold the legendary Jesus in no wise responsible for the trouble: it began with Luther, perhaps, and went on with Wesley; but no matter! — what I am trying to get at is the religion which makes England to-day a hell for any man who cares at all for freedom. That religion they call Christianity; the devil they honour they call God. I accept these definitions, as a poet must do, if he is to be at all intelligible to his age, and it is their God and their religion that I hate and will destroy.

THE POEM ITSELF

I should really leave this to my friend Captain Fuller to dissect at his leisure, that he might bye-and-bye edify the public in a little monograph of say 350,000 words. But it seems to me important to explain the form to a reader before he begins. For the work so transcends my own critical faculties that I am sure others will find difficulty in getting my point of view without very serious attention.

In the first place, my predecessor Shelley was so naturally gentle that his Prometheus can be read to-day by our young ladies without their ever suspecting that he was getting at God.

Nietzsche on the other hand is very obscure, very superficial, very philosophical, and he did not write English.

I have been trained in a harder school than Shelley; and so my little finger is thicker than my father's loins. He went and "trod the glaciers of the Alps" — the Mer de Glace; I broke the record by my 68 days on the Baltoro glacier. He went out in a boat, and got drowned at that; I have travelled on the Bralduh in a Zak. He shrank from the sight of a butcher's shop; I followed wounded buffalo into the jungle on foot. He thought Indians were "mild"; I shot two Bengalis. He never had such a galaxy of imbecility before him as R.J. Campbell, Winnington-Ingram, Tolstoy, Bernard Vaughan, Torrey, Dowie, Bernard Shaw, Booth, Father Ignatius, and my Uncle Tom.

He had not read the Encyclical against Modernism; the religious essays of the Right Hon. W.E. Gladstone, and the preposterous Balfour. He was unfamiliar with the spermatorrhoea of Tennyson's thought, and the diarrhoea of its simulacrum in G.K. Chesterton.

This explains why Shelley's wholesome indignation appears in me as little less than a blind lust of Destruction. (That is to say, on the rare occasion when I so far fall from adeptship as to credit the evidence of my senses).

I have consequently done all I can to shock and hurt the enemy. I have painted their God as the obscene thing he is from my knowledge of my Uncle Tom; I have made his Trinity ridiculous and his scheme disgusting; I have painted Magdalen as the Syrian strumpet she was from the best models among English society

whores (thank you, Ada; thank you, Kathleen!); I have painted
Mary as a lascivious flapper from my knowledge of English virgins
— thank you, Vera! thank you, Lydia! thank you, Millicent! — the
hag is my mother-in-law, and the baboon the Reverend F.F. Kelly.
I cannot pretend to remember exactly who 'sat' for the ox and the
ass, though the names of Charles Watts and Joseph McCabe
somehow instinctively suggest themselves in this connection. The
satyr and nymph crowd are mostly painted from imagination, for
on my honour I hardly know so many decent people; I painted
Jesus first as a joke — the brass bottle of our braying clergy; I
developed him as a low class Jew (not knowing any South African
millionnaires I took him straight out of the Gospel) and lastly I
miraculously turned him into a real man chiefly out of compliment
to the distinguished fictionist Ernest Renan. In other words, I
have kept as close to my documents as any one has any reason to
expect.

With regard to the plot, I must ask my readers to believe in the
existence of a great magical brotherhood formal or informal
pledged to the guardianship of mankind.

With this postulate the way is clear.

In the prologue we find innocence: Pagan love, Pagan music,
Pagan mysticism, and we find the Sabbatarians pretty sick about
it, like the fox that lost his tail.

We next find Alexander, one of the guardians, anxious about
humanity. He is not squeamish about a little blood, his own or
another's, and he discovers the plot.

Next we find the dove achieving his foul purpose, not on a pure
laughing Pagan girl, but on a furtive lecherous girl, already half a
Christian. Enough of this painful subject!

Now comes the Nativity, with the guardians, under Alexander's
presidency, on the watch. They are perfectly indifferent to all but
the secret purpose — more magical ethics, my disciples! They are
moved neither to pity nor to disgust, for the Great Pity and the
Great Disgust have moved them to this Immobility.

Next we see love under Christianity, as guilt, disease, weariness;
and the half-man rotted by its revolting filth, consenting to the
ruin of mankind and his own death as relief from it.

Lastly we see the man magically awakened to a sense of his

disaster, too weak to retrieve the past or avert the future, though alive to all its horror. In the meanwhile the corruption of Roman virtue begins; and we should end the play in despair were it not that Alexander comes forward and obligingly prophesies the arrival of Aleister Crowley — the Saviour of the Earth. So that the reader need only turn back to the title-page to see that the Light hath indeed arisen in darkness.

THE ENGLISH SPIRIT

It was in my mind to discourse freely upon this engaging topic; but to say truth I am somewhat weary, having now written for some six hours, and being well assured that if I once laid down the pen nothing would persuade me to resume the distasteful task. For there is no ecstasy in argument and exposition as there is in Poetry. That is why journalists are such dull dogs, even when they start as brilliant men. My readers, too, may be weary. They may say to me, as Lord Tankerville said to me at eleven A.M. on the 7th of July 1907, "I'm sick of your teaching — teaching — teaching — as if you were God Almighty and I were a poor bloody shit in the street!" —

I could not blame them.

On the whole, too, I cannot see that I have left much unsaid in the poem — which was written long ago when I lived, as will be obvious from the style, in Paddington. I will therefore beg my readers to proceed to the same and thence to the work itself; and leave the Bal Bullier and his Dorothy to their glad work of restoring the victim of British stupidity — else why these miles of preface? — weary Aleister Crowley, to his Pagan rapture.

PROEM

Master, I come. but ere the pregnant gloom
Lighten at last, I ask myself for whom
I take the pen, since English throbs and glows
Forth from its gold, like streams from sunny snows.
And if I write for England, who will read?
As if, when moons of Ramazan recede,
Some fatuous angel-porter should deposit
His perfect wine within the privy closet!
"What do they know, who only England know?"
Only what England paints its face to show.
Love mummied and relabelled "chaste affection,"
And lust excused as "natural selection."
Caligula upbraids the cruel cabby,
And Nero birches choir-boys in the Abbey:
Semiramis sandpapered to a simper,
And Clytemnaestra whittled to a whimper!
The austerities of Loyola? to seek!
But — let us have a "self-denial week!"
The raptures of Teresa are hysteric;
But — let us giggle at some fulsome cleric!
"The age refines! You lag behind." God knows!
Plus ca change, plus c'est la meme chose.
That Crowley knows you as you are — that frets.
He buys no doctored dung for violets!

XXXV

Your smug content, your Puritan surprise,
All lies, and lies; all lies, and lies, and lies!
Pathics from Eton, ever on ther knees,
Amazed at their twin brothers the Chinese!
Pathics from Harrow, reaking of Patchouli,
Shocked at the vice of the Mongolian coolie!
Canons of Westminster, with boy-rape sterile,
Hope Christ may save us from the Yellow Peril!
To call forced labour slavery is rude,
"Terminologic inexactitude."
This from the masters of the winds and waves
Whose cotton-mills are crammed with British slaves!
Men pass their nights with German-Jewish whores,
Their days in keeping "aliens" from our shores.
They turn their eyes up at a Gautier's tale,
And run a maisonette in Maida Vale.
Murder poor Wakley — the assassin leaves
Escorted by the Yard's blackmailing thieves,
Lest dead men (or their papers) should tell tales
And maybe compromise the Prince of Wales.
Arrest poor Wilde — the creaking Channel tubs
Groan with the consternation of the Clubs.
Scared, hushed, and pale, our men of eminence
Wait the result in sickening suspense.
Announced, all Mayfair shrieks its decent joy;
And, feeling safe, goes out and hires a boy.
Your titles — oh! how proud you are to wear them?
— What about "homo quatuor literarum?"
The puissant all their time to vice devote;
The impotent (contented) pay to gloat.
The strumpet's carwheels splash the starving maiden
In Piccadilly, deadlier than Aden.
"England expects a man to do his duty."
He calls truth lies, and sneers at youth and beauty,
Pays cash for love and fancies he has won it —

Duty means church, where he thanks God he's done it!
Morley's Hotel is the one stance to see
Our Nelson from! — Oh God! that I should be
Alone among this slime! — I saw Thy Graal:
Show me the men that have not bowed to Baal!
For as I love with spirit and with sense
I nauseate at this crawling crapulence,
Our whole state, summed in one supreme enigma,
Solved (in a second) by a simple Σ
Monstrous conjunctions with black man and brute
Level our ladies with the prostitute:
Our spinsters chaste in criminal abortion,
And matron with the pox for marriage portion;
Husbands who pimp all day for their young wives,
Athletes from Oxford, pathic all their lives,
Who sport the "so" coat, the sotadic necktie,
And lisp their filthy pun "Mens conscia recti!"
Priest who are celibates — outside of choir!
Maidens who rave in Lesbian desire:
The buck of sixty, cunning as a trapper,
Stalking the pig-tailed, masturbating flapper;
The creeping Jesus — Caution! we may shock it! —
With one hand through his torn-out breeches pocket;
Flagellants shrieking in our streets and schools,
Our men all hogs, and all our women ghouls: —
This is our England, pious dame and prude,
Who calls me blasphemous, unchaste, and rude!
Come to sweet air, poor sirens of the stews!
A pox on all these yammering Yahoos!
My healthy sperm begets the Son of God
Winged with the dawn and with the star-stream shod!
Not on your purulence and ichorous itch,
O English girl, half baby and half bitch,
But on the glorious body and soul of her
Of whom I am the Lord and worshipper,

The brave gay cleanly maiden whose embrace
Flushes with shameless fervour the fair face,
Fills the whole leaping heaven with the light
Till all the world is drunken with delight.
You with your own authentic filth defiled
Robbed Keats of life, and Shelley of his child,
Corrupted Swinburn to your foul disease,
Denied Blake bread — are you fed full on these?
You hate the wise, true, beautiful, and holy: —
Dogs! is there nothing you can do to Crowley?

....

Therefore I see and speak, who would be dumb
And blind: but Thou dost call. Master, I come,

ALEISTER CROWLEY.

THE PERSONS OF THE PROLOGUE

SATYRS
- Marsyas
- Silenus
- Chiron

NYMPHS
- Chrysis
- Doris
- Atthis

GIRLS
- Rhodope
- Erinna
- Evadne

YOUNG BOYS
- Antinous
- Giton
- Hylas

MEN
- Anaximander
- Lysander
- Anaxagoras

HERMAPHRODITES
- Rhodon
- Salmacis
- Erotion

FAUNS
- Heliorus
- Hyacinthus
- Olympas

OTHERS
Heracleitus, a philospher
Chrysippus, his disciple
Yaugh Waugh, a man vulture
A lambkin
A dove

THE PERSONS OF THE TRAGEDY

Alexander, a wise king, ruling Macedon, Babylonia, etc.
Two Saytrs
A fair man child
Two nymphs
Miriam, a Syrian Girl
A white robed youth
Legions of apes, worms, and monsters
Agrippa, a Roman Century
Publius, his lieutenant
A Roman guard
A hag
A blue faced baboon
An ox
Zakariah, an ass
Govinda, kind of the Indines
Chau, Son of Heaven, king of Tartary and China
A company of rats
A company of toads
A brass bottle containing a mannikin in blue
Issa, the grown man thereof
Magda, an odalisque
John, a young scrible
Bystanders